BRIGHT
IDEA
BOOKS

KWAME
Alexander

by Abby Cooper

CAPSTONE PRESS
a capstone imprint

Bright Idea Books are published by Capstone Press
1710 Roe Crest Drive, North Mankato, Minnesota 56003
www.mycapstone.com

Library of Congress Cataloging-in-Publication Data
Library of Congress Cataloging-in-Publication Date is available on the Library of Congress website.
ISBN: 978-1-5435-5792-3 (library hardcover)
978-1-5435-6037-4 (paperback)
978-1-5435-5824-1 (eBook PDF)

Editorial Credits
Editor: Claire Vanden Branden
Designer: Becky Daum
Production Specialist: Colleen McLaren

Quote Source
p. 4, "Newbery Medal Acceptance Speech." *ALSC*, 2015

Photo Credits
Alamy: ZUMA Press, Inc./Alamy, 16; AP Images: Andrew Wardlow/The News Herald, 19, Matt Sayles, cover; Getty Images: Katherine Frey/The Washington Post, 25; Newscom: Birdie Thompson/AdMedia, 5, 28, Johnny Louis/JL/Sipa USA, 23; Rex Features: Matt Sayles/AP, 26; Shutterstock Images: Anna Sheppard, 6–7, 8, 14–15, Anutr Yossundara, 30–31, atm2003, 20–21, Maks Ershov, 11; Yearbook Library: Yearbook Library, 13

Printed in the United States of America.
PA48

TABLE OF CONTENTS

CHAPTER 1

BEING
Kwame

"Write a poem that is **contagious**. Let it **inspire**," Kwame Alexander said. He had ended his speech. The crowd clapped. He had just won the Newbery Medal. He won it for his book *The Crossover*. Alexander was happy. The book had taken five years to write. He had worked very hard.

Kwame Alexander enjoys writing for kids of all ages.

THE JOHN NEWBERY MEDAL

The John Newbery Medal is an award given out each year. It is for the best American books for children.

The Crossover is told through poetry. It is about twin brothers who play basketball. They are 12 years old. Alexander wrote about what had mattered to him at that age. He wrote about sports, family, and friends.

The Crossover was very successful. This led Alexander to write a book related to *The Crossover* titled *Rebound*.

Alexander attended a book fair with award-winning author James Patterson (right) in 2018.

Kids of all ages read *The Crossover*.
They love it. Adults do, too. The book
has won many awards.

CHAPTER 2

AWARD-WINNING Writer

Alexander was born on August 21, 1950. He was born in New York. He grew up around books. His father **published** them. His mother taught English.

Alexander grew up in Manhattan, New York.

11

Alexander started writing when he was 12. He wrote a Mother's Day poem. It made his mother happy. He learned more about poetry in college. Later, he wrote poems for his wife. Alexander kept writing. He has not stopped since.

FIRST NAME

Kwame is Alexander's middle name. His first name is Edward.

Alexander was a member of the newspaper staff in junior high.

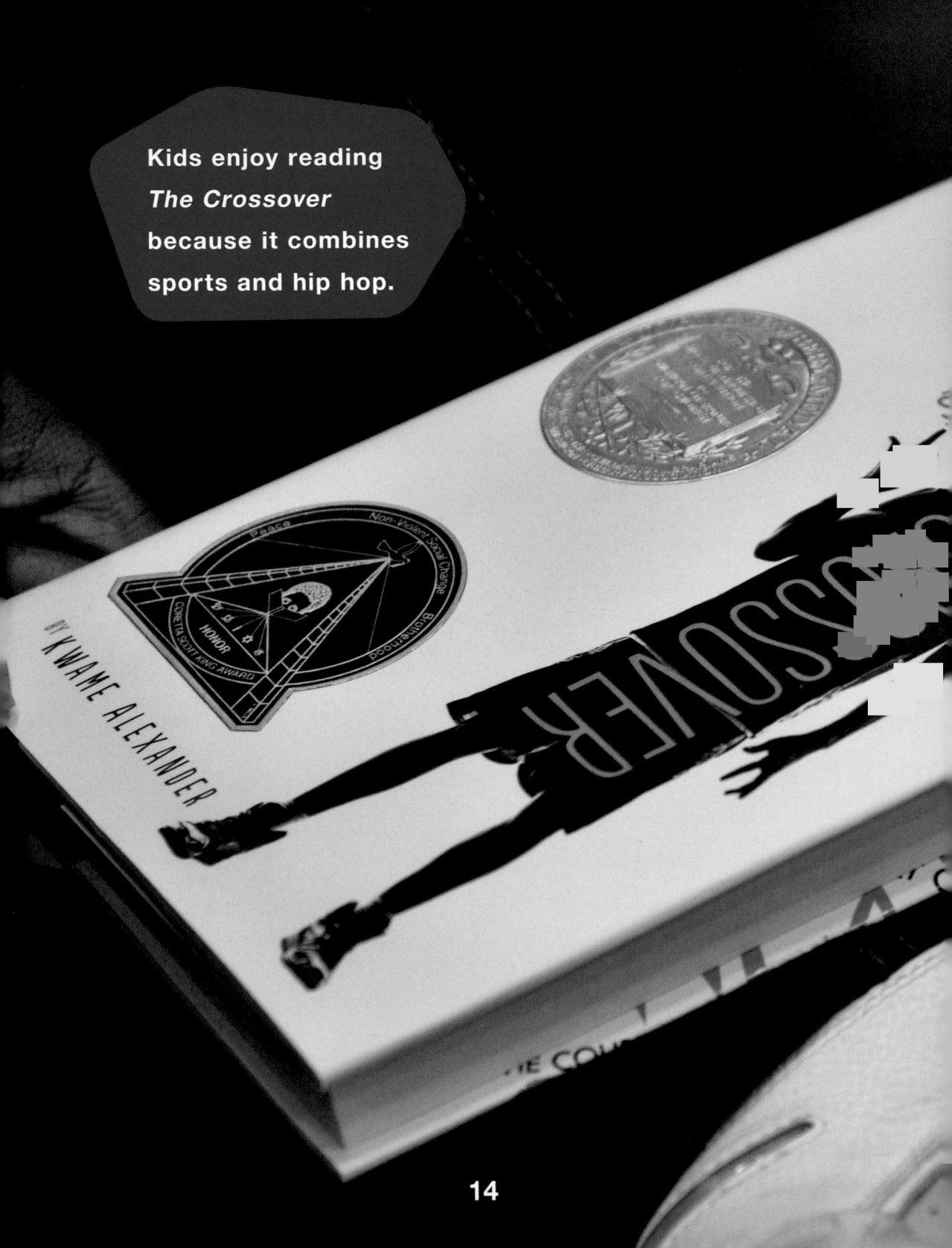

Kids enjoy reading *The Crossover* because it combines sports and hip hop.

BIG SUCCESS

Alexander has written more than 20 books. He writes for children and adults. He is best known for *The Crossover*. It came out in 2014.

But Alexander's road to success was not easy. Publishers turned down *The Crossover* more than 20 times. They didn't think kids wanted a book about poetry and sports. They were wrong. Finally a publisher agreed to print the book. It became a big success.

Alexander's book *Solo* was published in 2017.

Alexander wrote more books about poetry and sports. His books are also about family, friendship, and love. His list of books continues to grow.

BEST SELLERS

Alexander has written six best-selling books.

CHAPTER 3

LENDING a Hand

Alexander likes to help others. So he started Book-in-a-Day in 2006. The program taught students about writing and publishing. Students left with a strong piece of writing. Book-in-a-Day ran for nine years.

Alexander still helps kids. He does this in many ways. He visits schools and libraries. He travels the country. He meets as many kids as he can. He has a positive impact on everyone he meets.

When Alexander visits schools, he helps students get excited about reading.

LEAP for Ghana helps children in Ghana, Africa.

LEAP FOR GHANA

In 2012, Alexander created LEAP for Ghana. He did this with writer Tracy Chiles McGhee. LEAP for Ghana helps African kids and adults. The program brings books and schooling to people who need them. On its first trip, the group built a library. Alexander continues to travel to Ghana. He makes a difference in communities near and far.

HEALTH CARE

LEAP for Ghana also brings health services to people who need them.

CHAPTER 4

LOOKING
Ahead

Alexander leads a busy life. He writes, speaks, and travels. He spends time with his wife and daughters. He comes up with new projects.

Alexander attends many book fairs where he talks to audiences about writing.

In 2017, Alexander started an online show called *Bookish*. He talks to other writers on the show. He also continues to write new books. His book *Rebound* was published in 2018.

Alexander also makes music based on his books. He works with his friend Randy Preston. They have even made music videos.

Alexander loves talking to kids about his books.

Alexander wants to publish books from people whose voices have never been heard.

A BIG IDEA

Alexander wanted more people to tell stories. In 2018, he created an **imprint** called Versify. Many of the books are also written with poetry. Alexander wants to publish books that touch kids.

GLOSSARY

contagious
spread from one person
to another

imprint
a brand name under which
books are published

inspire
fill someone with the urge
to do something or feel
something creative

publish
to prepare and issue a book
for public sale

TIMELINE

1950: Kwame Alexander is born on August 21 in New York City, New York.

1993: Alexander's first book is published.

2012: Alexander starts LEAP for Ghana.

2015: Alexander's book *The Crossover* wins the John Newbery Medal.

2018: Alexander starts his own imprint, Versify, at Houghton Mifflin Harcourt Books for Young Readers.

ACTIVITY

Poetry is very important in Alexander's books and in his life. Now, it's your turn to give poetry a try. Create your own poems using some of the same styles Alexander uses in his books.

To write an acrostic poem, pick a word, such as your name or favorite animal. Write the word vertically. Then, next to each letter, write another word that begins with the letter and describes your first word.

A list poem can be a list of people, places, items, or ideas. List poems are often funny when writers include things that are unexpected or unusual.

Free verse poems do not follow any rules. They can be whatever the writer wants. Choose a topic, put your pencil on the paper, and let the words flow!

FURTHER RESOURCES

Want to get to know Alexander even better? Enjoy these interviews:

Kwame's Frequently Asked Questions
http://kwamealexander.com/about/me/c/199

Reading Rockets
http://www.readingrockets.org/books/interviews/alexander/transcript

Sports Illustrated Kids
https://www.sikids.com/si-kids/2016/01/12/author-interview-kwame-alexander

Ready to learn more about Alexander's other projects? Check this out:

LEAP for Ghana
http://www.leapglobal.org/

McGrath, Brian S. *Game Changers: Kwame Alexander.* Huntington Beach, CA: Teacher Created Materials, 2017.

INDEX

7

BRIGHT IDEA BOOKS

Kwame Alexander's book, *The Crossover*, won several awards. His books combine poetry, sports, and rap. Learn how he encourages kids to read!

BOOKS IN THIS SERIES

Amandla Stenberg
Barack Obama
Dwayne Johnson
Jordan Peele
Karlie Kloss
Kwame Alexander
Marley Dias
Storm Reid

capstone
www.mycapstone.com

MILLIE BOBBY
Brown

by Martha London

INFLUENTIAL PEOPLE

Bright Ideas is published by Capstone Press, an imprint of Capstone.
1710 Roe Crest Drive
North Mankato, Minnesota 56003
www.capstonepub.com

Library of Congress Cataloging-in-Publication Data
Names: London, Martha, author.
Title: Millie Bobby Brown / Martha London.
Description: North Mankato : Capstone Press, 2020. | Series: Influential People | Includes bibliographical references and index. | Audience: Grades 4-6
Identifiers: LCCN 2019029510 (print) | LCCN 2019029511 (ebook) | ISBN 9781543590821 (hardcover) | ISBN 9781496665881 (paperback) | ISBN 9781543590838 (ebook)
Subjects: LCSH: Brown, Millie Bobby, 2004—Juvenile literature. | Actors—United States Biography—Juvenile literature.
Classification: LCC PN2287.B724 L66 2010 (print) | LCC PN2287.B724 (ebook) | DDC 791.4502/8092 [B]—dc23
LC record available at https://lccn.loc.gov/2019029510
LC ebook record available at https://lccn.loc.gov/2019029511

Image Credits
Alamy: Daren Fentiman/Zuma Press, Inc., 23, PictureLux/The Hollywood Archive, 19; AP Images: Chris Pizzello/Invision, cover; Getty Images: Frederick M. Brown/Getty Images Entertainment, 17, Kevork Djansezian/BAFTA LA/Getty Images Entertainment, 9; iStockphoto: asiseeit, 31; Rex Features: Lodovico Colli Di Felizzano/WWD, 20, Rob Latour, 13, Stewart Cook, 10, Shutterstock Images: CarlaVanWagoner, 6–7, Dfree, 5, Jstone, 26–27, Kathy Hutchins, 14, lev radin, 24
Design Elements: Shutterstock Images

Editorial Credits
Editor: Charly Haley; Designer: Laura Graphenteen; Production Specialist: Colleen McLaren

Quote Source
p. 26, "Millie Bobby Brown Supported the March for Our Lives with a Jean Jacket and Passionate Speech," *W*, March 25, 2018.

All internet sites appearing in back matter were available and accurate when this book was sent to press.

Printed in the United States of America.
PA99

TABLE OF CONTENTS

CHAPTER 1

A YOUNG
Star

The director yells, "Cut!" Millie Bobby Brown leaves the stage. She is not needed for the next scene. But Millie loves watching the other actors. She sneaks back onstage. Millie hides behind a chair. She watches as the crew films.

Millie Bobby Brown at the premiere of *Stranger Things* season 3 in 2019

Millie is an actor. She is on the TV show *Stranger Things*. She got a lead **role** when she was 11 years old. Her character was quiet at first. But her facial **expressions** told a story. Millie and the show received a lot of praise. *Stranger Things* gave Millie other opportunities.

Millie loves acting. But she is also an **activist**. Millie helps kids. She wants every kid to feel safe. Her fame makes people listen. Millie works to make a difference.

CHAPTER 2

GROWING Up

Millie was born on February 19, 2004.

She has two sisters and one brother.

Her parents are British.

Millie moved a lot. She was born in Spain. Her family moved to the United Kingdom when Millie was 4. They moved again in 2011. This time they moved to Florida. Millie loved acting. She took classes on Saturdays. Millie practiced in a studio with other young actors.

Millie and her dad in 2014

9

Millie used to watch TV to learn from the actors. Now millions of people watch her on TV.

A Hollywood **talent scout** saw Millie perform. The scout told Millie's parents she was talented. She said Millie had good **instincts**. The scout said Millie could be successful.

LEARNING ON HER OWN

Millie was born in Europe. But she speaks with an American **accent**. She taught herself the accent by watching American TV.

A YOUNG ACTOR

Millie's parents supported her acting. They did not have a lot of money. But they wanted Millie to follow her dreams.

Millie always dreamed of being an actor.

13

Millie (right) met many people to work with in Los Angeles.

Millie's family moved to Los Angeles, California. This gave Millie more opportunities to act. Her parents drove her to meetings. Millie met a lot of **agents**. The agents helped her find acting roles. Millie **auditioned** for different parts. Some were for movies. Some were for TV shows. Millie did not care what role she got. She just wanted to act.

CHAPTER 3

FINDING
Fame

Millie found TV roles quickly. In 2013 she played young Alice in *Once Upon a Time in Wonderland*. She was in two episodes. She later had small roles in *NCIS* and *Grey's Anatomy*.

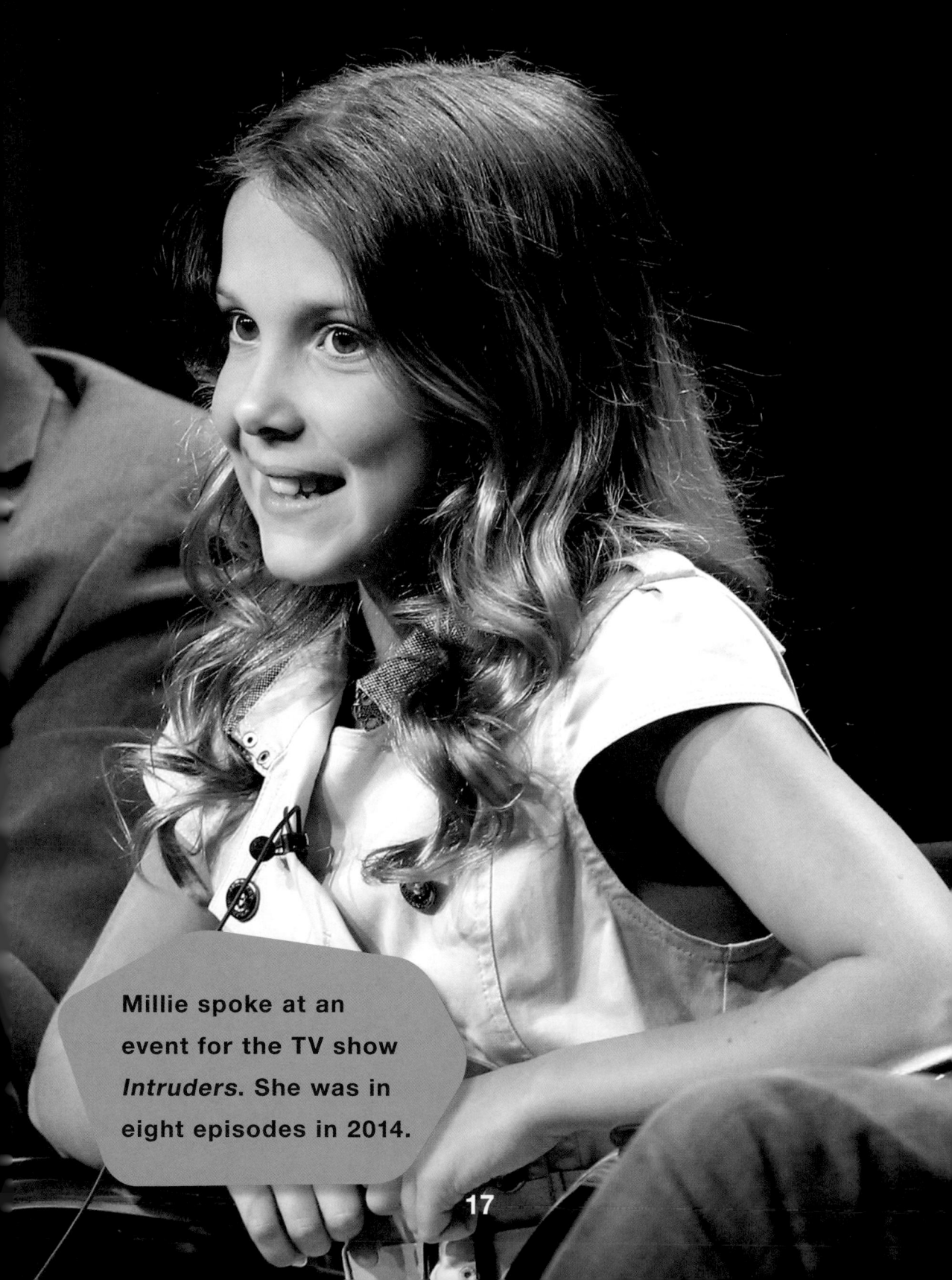

Millie spoke at an event for the TV show *Intruders*. She was in eight episodes in 2014.

17

HER BIG BREAK

Millie's career took off in 2016. She was **cast** as Eleven in the Netflix show *Stranger Things*. She had to shave her head. Millie was not afraid to be bald. She did what she needed to do for her role. She wanted to be great.

Stranger Things became really popular. Millie was a star.

Millie (center-right) in a scene from *Stranger Things*

Millie (right) with model Naomi Campbell at Milan Fashion Week in 2018

Soon Millie started to do more than acting. She starred in a fashion **campaign** in 2017. She was also in her first music video. The video was for the band Sigma.

MUSICAL TALENT

Millie likes music. She can sing and rap.

CHAPTER 4

TRUE TO
Herself

Millie had become famous. But sometimes being famous can be hard. People can be mean. They are even mean to famous people like Millie.

People spread **rumors** about Millie. They said she was a bad role model. Some people told her to dress differently. Millie took down her Twitter account after being bullied. She tries to not listen to hurtful comments. She wants to stay true to herself.

Even when she speaks at events, Millie likes to be herself.

Millie is one of the youngest actors to ever work with UNICEF.

MAKING A DIFFERENCE

Millie wants to make the world a better place. She uses her fame to make a difference. She works with UNICEF. It is an organization that helps kids. Millie fights for kids' education and safety. She wants to end bullying and school shootings.

OUTSIDE OF FAME

Millie works hard. But she also takes time to do things for fun. Millie enjoys practicing **boxing**.

Millie knows people will listen to her. She speaks about what she believes. She said in a speech, "I'm privileged to have a voice that can be heard, one that I can use to hopefully make a positive difference."

While Millie works to help people, she also likes to have fun.

GLOSSARY

accent
a way people from a certain country or region often speak

activist
a person who works for social or political change

agent
a person who helps actors find work

audition
to try out for a part in a show or play

boxing
a fighting sport that involves punching a bag or a partner

campaign
a series of photos and videos to advertise a brand

cast
called to play a certain role

expression
the way a person's face looks to show an emotion

instinct
a feeling for how or when to do something

role
a part in a TV show, movie, or play

rumor
an often untrue statement meant to hurt a person

talent scout
a person who looks for people to become actors

TIMELINE

2004: Millie Bobby Brown is born on February 19.

2011: Millie's family moves to Florida.

2013: Millie gets a role in *Once Upon a Time in Wonderland*.

2016: Millie gets the role of Eleven in *Stranger Things*.

2017: Millie stars in her first music video.

2018: Millie begins working with UNICEF.

ACTIVITY

MAKE A VIDEO

Millie Bobby Brown loved to act from a young age. She took classes in her community. These classes helped prepare her for life as an actor. But you don't need classes to practice acting.

Get a group of your friends together and create a short video. You could even start your own TV series. You don't need fancy equipment. Any smartphone will work. Your library or school may have a smartphone or camera that you can borrow. When the video is finished, you can watch it together. Invite your friends and family to see your work.

FURTHER RESOURCES

Interested in learning more about Millie? Check out this book:

Orr, Nicole K. *Millie Bobby Brown*. Kennett Square, Penn.: Purple Toad Publishing, 2018.

Are you interested in acting? Check out these resources:

Bell, Samantha S. *You Can Work in Movies*. North Mankato, Minn.: Capstone Press, 2019.

Rauf, Don. *Choose Your Own Career Adventure in Hollywood*. Ann Arbor, Mich.: Cherry Lake Publishing, 2017.

Wonderopolis: Can Anyone Be an Actor?
https://wonderopolis.org/wonder/can-anyone-be-an-actor

Wonderopolis: How Do You Become Famous?
https://wonderopolis.org/wonder/how-do-you-become-famous

INDEX

7